THE LIFE-CHANGING MAGIC OF
BAKING

A
**BEGINNER'S
GUIDE**
BY
JOY THE BAKER

JOY WILSON

WITH **CLIFF WILSON**

MAGIC CAT 🐱 PUBLISHING

NEW YORK

HI, I'M JOY.

I'm here to tell you how baking changed my life . . .
and share the magic of baking with you too.

I GREW UP WATCHING MY PARENTS BAKE.

Our oven was small, so if Mom was making a cake at the same time that Dad was making a pie, Dad would wait until Mom's cake was out of the oven before he rolled out his pie crust.

On my fifth birthday, Mom traced the outline of my hand on paper.

She used it to make my hand into a mini-cake! It went on top of my big birthday cake.

I felt like I had done something important.

At the end of this book, I'm going to show you how you and your grown-up can make your own special cake together!

In this book, I'm going to talk about the equipment I use in my kitchen, so let's have a quick look at some of it . . .

For measuring your ingredients:

LIQUID MEASURING CUP

MEASURING SPOONS AND CUPS

KITCHEN SCALE

For mixing your ingredients:

MIXING BOWL AND SPOON

STAND MIXER

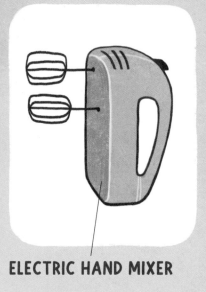

ELECTRIC HAND MIXER

(AND YOUR ARM MUSCLES!)

For cooking your ingredients:

OVEN MITTS

COOKIE SHEET

CAKE PANS

OVEN

Ovens get **HOT**, so always have a grown-up with you when you bake!

Don't forget—always wash your hands in warm, soapy water before you start.

When I was young, I was allowed to measure out ingredients and try fun tasks like cracking eggs or sifting flour.

I also had to wash dishes, which wasn't as much fun!

Baking continued to be part of my life as I grew up.

I want to go for a job in a bakery!

I told my parents my plans while we munched on Dad's chocolate chip cookies.

Well, why don't you make a batch of these cookies and take them to your job interview?

I made the dough and dotted each cookie with extra chocolate chips.

Then I baked them . . .

and took them to my interview.

And wouldn't you know it? I got the job! I was a professional baker!

I started writing about baking online, too, calling myself "Joy the Baker."

People liked what I wrote, and now I share my recipes and my love of baking with hundreds of thousands of people all round the world.

This dish is simply amazing!

This was delicious!!!

The texture and flavor are perfect!

I even have my own Joy the Baker cookbooks and magazines.

So—let me tell you exactly how I got here, and how you can learn to bake like me too!

#1 BAKING TOGETHER IS DOUBLE THE FUN!

I loved having sleepovers with my friends when I was a kid.

At my tenth birthday sleepover, I wanted to give cupcakes to all my friends.

Dad helped me.

He **creamed** the butter and sugar.

I added the eggs, vanilla, and cream cheese.

After mixing in the flour and baking powder, we put the cupcakes in the oven.

When they came out, they were golden and soft to touch. Then we added frosting when they'd cooled.

After my friends sang "Happy Birthday" to me, I smiled at Dad. We'd had a great time baking together!

Creaming is when soft butter and sugar are blended together. Two things happen when you cream butter and sugar.

One, the ingredients are combined.

Two, a fluffy mixture is created.

You can use a stand mixer . . .

an electric hand mixer . . .

or your bowl, spoon, and arm muscles!

Keep creaming until the butter and sugar become slightly pale in color and very fluffy in texture.

The fluffiness is air worked into the butter and sugar.

The air will help your cake bake up soft and tall!

BAKING A CAKE IS LIKE BUILDING A HOUSE

Dad taught me that **eight** ingredients are basic for most cakes:

1. flour
2. sugar
3. eggs
4. a fat, like butter or oil
5. a dairy ingredient, such as milk or cream cheese (or a non-dairy alternative)
6. a raising agent, like baking powder or baking soda (or sometimes both)
7. a pinch of salt

And the eighth ingredient . . .? **Heat!**

The way that each of these ingredients works in a recipe is like how a house is built.

FLOUR makes up the foundation of the house and the bricks

BAKING POWDER is the cement that goes between the bricks

OIL is the plumbing that keeps everything flowing and moist

EGGS are the beams that support the roof

Isn't that neat?

SUGAR is the window that lets in the light

SALT is the furniture that makes the house complete

MILK is the paint that covers the walls

HEAT is the electricity that makes everything run

TAKE THE TIME TO PREPARE

Every baker in a professional kitchen gathers and measures ingredients before baking a recipe.

Taking your time equals baking success. You wouldn't want to bake a cake and discover that it's dry and crumbly because you forgot to put in milk!

One thing I like to do is separate my ingredients into three groups, as it makes following a recipe much easier.

Ingredients for **creaming**

BUTTER SUGAR Vanilla

Dry ingredients (apart from sugar)

BAKING POWDER BAKING SODA FLOUR COCOA 100% GROUND CINNAMON SALT

Dairy ingredients (or **non-dairy** alternatives)

CREAM CHEESE MILK CREAM COCONUT MILK

Taking your time as you measure out ingredients is important too. Too much or too little of something might make a recipe turn out a different way.

Here are some words you might see in a recipe that mean different types of measurement.

ounces (oz)   grams (g)

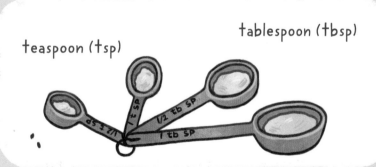

teaspoon (tsp)   tablespoon (tbsp)

1/2 t sp   1 t sp   1/2 tb sp   1 tb sp

cup (c)   milliliters (ml)

1 cup

#4 PRACTICE, PRACTICE, PRACTICE!

Baking, like any skill, takes lots and lots of practice.

Everybody makes mistakes, but when you finish what you start, you have accomplished something, no matter the results.

You can keep practicing until you achieve even better results.

Many times, even with mistakes, your ingredients will have done their hard work to create a treat.

But other times, what you pull out of the oven is flat, burned, and dry.

Here are a couple of tips I give bakers who run into problems, to help them next time they bake.

Help, Joy! My cookies are flat!

Chill your dough in the fridge for one hour before making your cookies.

Cookies become flat because the butter in the dough has melted too quickly, but **cold** butter in the dough will melt less quickly, allowing the cookies to rise.

Help, Joy! My cake sank in the center!

Let a cake bake until it's *almost* done before opening the oven or moving the pan.

A cake can sink if you open the oven and move the pan during those important first 20 minutes of baking.

The cake is still fragile, so moving or rotating the pan can cause your cake to collapse.

You can always learn from your mistakes. Even flops can be delicious!

DON'T IGNORE THE SMALL STUFF

Every recipe is both a list of ingredients and a friendly guide on how to bring them together.

It might seem like some of the instructions in a recipe are unimportant . . .

Whisk for 45 seconds . . .

1/2 teaspoon of baking soda . . .

or too small to really matter.

But don't be tempted to ignore things that don't seem important. The little details are not for nothing.

Amazing Cakes

If a recipe says that some ingredients need to be at **room temperature**, it's because the right temperature helps create the right scientific reactions in the oven.

Room temperature means taking ingredients out of the fridge to get warmer.

If butter smooshes slightly when you press it with the back of a spoon, and if an eggshell no longer has a chill, that's room temperature.

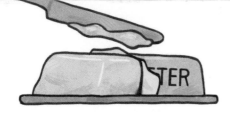

Butter needs to be at room temperature so that it can **cream** with sugar.

Eggs will **fluff up** better in the oven when they are added in at room temperature.

If a recipe says to **whisk dry ingredients together** before adding liquid ingredients, it's because **whisking** dry ingredients first will help ensure everything is mixed in equally.

Properly mixed-in baking soda will help the cake rise evenly in the oven.

Properly mixed-in salt or spices means the cake will taste perfect, whichever side you take a slice from!

#6 PATIENCE IS AN INGREDIENT TOO!

Baking sometimes requires lots of waiting. When I was a young baker, I would stare through the oven window, waiting and waiting, wondering when my cake would start to rise!

Remember . . .

Patience is the secret ingredient in every recipe.

So while you are waiting and your mouth is watering, why not . . .

do some drawing,

or play with friends,

or wash the dishes!

Here are some tasty reasons why you need **patience** as a baker.

Cookie dough needs to chill in the refrigerator first so the ingredients can get used to each other and become friends.

An **apple pie** has to cool for several hours for the juices to thicken.

A **cake** is done when you poke a skewer into the center and just a few crumbs are left on the skewer when you pull it out.

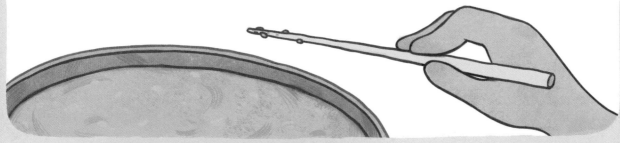

One of the first things I learned to do in the kitchen was **cracking eggs**.

I had to take it slowly and gently, so I didn't get any pieces of eggshell in my cake batter!

Here's how to crack an egg with patience . . .

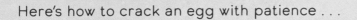

Gently tap the egg on the rim of your bowl to make a small crack in the shell.

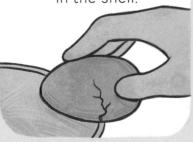

Carefully push your thumbs into the crack.

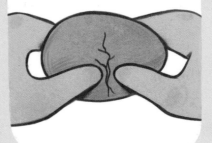

Slowly pull the two parts of the eggshell apart to let your egg fall into your bowl.

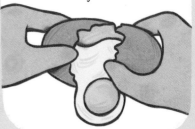

SEE IT THROUGH TO THE END

One thing I have learned as a baker is to always finish what I start.

Even when I've measured my ingredients and **greased and floured** the pan properly . . .

AND followed the instructions as best I can . . .

a batter or dough may be different from what I expected.

Sometimes baking can leave a big question mark in your head.

Why is it different?

Did I leave something out?

Will it turn out OK?

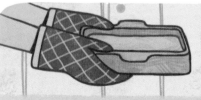

But no matter what, finish the recipe, put it in the oven . . .

and then use all of your patience as you wait to see what happens.

Greasing and flouring a pan ensures the cake will come out of the pan without sticking after it is baked!

Here's a **bundt cake**, which can be tricky to remove from its intricate mold!

When the instructions say to **grease**, you should use a paper towel to rub butter around the inside of your cake pan.

Then, to **flour** your pan, shake some flour around the pan to coat the butter.

Tap any excess out of the pan and into the garbage.

#8 GO ON A GOLDILOCKS ADVENTURE

As I grew up and was deciding what job I wanted, I went on what I call a "Goldilocks Adventure."

You know the story—where Goldilocks tries the bears' three bowls of porridge . . .

and one is too hot . . .

one is too cold . . .

and one is just right?

My too-hot bowl was a job as a cook in a diner in Miami, Florida.

It was SO fun and SO busy, but a bit too warm for me.

That busy kitchen made me sweaty!

My too-cold bowl was my time working in an ice cream shop in Vermont, where the winters are freezing cold.

The ice cream was delicious, though.

And then, I found my bowl that was just right . . .

I got a job in a bakery! I knew it was exactly where I belonged.

You don't have to be a grown-up to have a Goldilocks Adventure. Maybe yours will be finding a hobby you love or a sport to try.

You may need to try lots of things before you find something that is just right for you.

#9 IT TAKES A TEAM

Baking is great on your own,
but it's even more fun in a team!

One Thanksgiving, I had to make
hundreds of pies with my team
at the bakery.

A few days ahead of time, one baker
made all the pumpkin filling.

And I made the pie crusts
and froze them.

The day before Thanksgiving,
we started work at 2 a.m.!

Pumpkin filling was
poured into the crusts . . .

the pies were
put into a large oven . . .

and I took them out
when they were
perfectly baked!

As the sun rose, we enjoyed breakfast together while the pies cooled.

Then we all put the pies in boxes before our customers arrived.

It took a whole team to get those Thanksgiving pies ready on time!

At home, I like to decorate my Thanksgiving pie with whipped cream. Or I serve it with ice cream. That's called pie à la mode. Here are some other tasty decorations you could use to make any dessert look pretty!

FRUIT

NUTS

CHOCOLATE CHIPS

FROSTING

#10 PASS IT ON

When I started posting recipes on my blog, I realized how much I enjoyed sharing the thing that made me so happy.

I saw how excited that made *them*.

They would write to me about how delicious their freshly baked muffins or scones tasted.

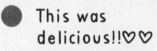

● **This was delicious!!♡♡**
1h   150 likes

● **Amaaazing!**
1h   72 likes

Then they would share my recipes with their friends.

You HAVE to try Joy's new recipe!

Yummy!

When a recipe is great, it's a treasure that you can pass on to spread the joy.

My dad's sweet potato pie is a tradition in our family every Thanksgiving.

Dad's recipe contains a combination of spices he's practiced and perfected throughout my childhood.

I shared it on my blog, and now Dad's pie is famous all around the world!

It's so cool to think some of my recipes have become tradition in families I've never even met.

That's the magic of baking. When we pass it on . . .

we help to create new memories and new traditions.

AND REMEMBER . . . LIFE IS ALWAYS JOYFUL WHEN YOU ADD SPRINKLES TO IT!

I put rainbow sprinkles on my toast in the morning if I wake up feeling a bit sad.

Could you add your own non-edible "sprinkles" to your day?

Maybe it could be giving yourself an extra-big smile when you look in the mirror . . .

or reminding yourself of something you're really good at.

Perhaps you could add sprinkles to someone else's day too.

There are chances for sprinkles everywhere, if you look for them!

You could say something nice to your teacher . . .

or give a friend a warm hug.

Offering a sincere compliment can make a difference.

It's an unexpected sprinkle of happiness you're giving to someone else!

BEFORE I GO . . .

What I learned in our family kitchen throughout my upbringing has helped shape me into who I am today.

Every day, I strive to show people how magical baking is.

I especially want to show readers like you how easy and fun it can be . . .

and of course, how tasty!

Baking will bring you joy, and it will help you bring joy
to others too. Baking really can be life-changing.

Don't be afraid of the kitchen—just roll up your sleeves,
tie up your apron, and . . .

HOW TO . . . BAKE JOY'S "HAPPY EVERY DAY" CAKE

Find your grown-up and let's bake my favorite cake together!

The recipe makes a 9-inch cake with two tasty layers!

For the Cake

- ½ cup (1 stick) unsalted butter, softened to room temperature, plus about 2 tablespoons more for greasing the pan
- 2¼ cups all-purpose flour, plus 1 tablespoon for flouring the pan
- 1½ cups sugar

- 3 large eggs, at room temperature
- 1 teaspoon pure vanilla extract
- 2 teaspoons baking powder
- 1 teaspoon baking soda
- 1 teaspoon salt
- 1¼ cups buttermilk*

* If you don't have buttermilk, you can mix 1 cup milk with 2 teaspoons lemon juice and 2 tablespoons plain yogurt and leave to stand for 10 minutes before using.

Instructions

1. Place a rack in the center of the oven and preheat the oven to 350°F. Grease and flour two 9-inch round cake pans. (Turn back to page 21 to remind yourself how!)
2. In the bowl of a stand mixer fitted with a paddle attachment (you can also use a large bowl and an electric hand mixer), cream together the butter and sugar until light and fluffy, about 3-5 minutes.
3. Stop the mixer and scrape down the sides of the bowl using a rubber spatula. Add one egg at a time, beating for 1 minute before each additional egg. Giving each egg special attention by mixing it for a full minute will ensure that the cake bakes up super fluffy.
4. Beat in the vanilla extract.
5. In a medium bowl, whisk together the flour, baking powder, baking soda, and salt. Add the dry ingredients all at once to the butter and egg mixture and beat on low until just combined. Then add the buttermilk and beat on low for 1 minute. Increase the speed to medium and beat for 3 minutes more. Start on a low speed so the buttermilk doesn't splash out of the bowl and make a big mess!
6. Pour the batter into the prepared pans. Bake for 25-30 minutes, or until the cake is cooked through and the top springs back lightly when touched. Some ovens run hotter than others so check for doneness after 22 minutes. It's ready when a skewer inserted in the center of the cake comes out with a few crumbs on it.
7. Remove from the oven and allow to cool in the pan for a few minutes, then remove the cakes to a wire rack and let them cool completely before frosting. A wire rack helps the cake layers cool on both top and bottom.

Now it's time for some frosting . . .

HOW TO . . . MAKE THE FROSTING FOR JOY'S "HAPPY EVERY DAY" CAKE

For the Chocolate Buttercream Frosting

- ¾ cup (1½ sticks) unsalted butter, softened to room temperature
- ½ cup unsweetened cocoa powder
- ¼ teaspoon salt
- 2½ cups powdered sugar
- 2 tablespoons whole milk
- 1 teaspoon pure vanilla extract
- ⅓ cup plus 1 tablespoon heavy cream
- ⅓ cup sweetened chocolate milk powder
- your choice of decorations, such as sprinkles, berries, writing icing, or anything else you like!

Instructions

1. Cream together the butter, cocoa powder, and salt in a stand mixer or using an electric whisk (or just your arm muscles). The butter mixture will be very thick. Turn off the mixer and scrape down the sides of the bowl using a rubber spatula.

2. Add the powdered sugar. Turn the mixer on low and blend in the powdered sugar while adding milk and vanilla extract. As the sugar combines with the other ingredients, increase the speed of the mixer to beat the frosting. Beat until smooth—about 1 minute. Start on low speed so the powdered sugar doesn't fly out of the bowl!

3. In a small bowl, stir together the heavy cream and chocolate milk powder. Turn the mixer speed to medium and add half of the heavy cream mixture into the frosting in a slow, steady stream. Stop the mixer and scrape down the sides of the bowl. Add the remaining cream mixture, or enough of it to reach your desired consistency. Beat until soft and creamy, about 1 minute.

4. Store in an airtight container in the refrigerator or freezer. It will set quite firm, so bring it to room temperature before using it.

5. Place the first layer of your cake on a plate and slather it generously with frosting—a palette knife is good for this. Carefully place the second layer on top and spread it with frosting. Decorate as you wish and happily eat a slice!

If it's a birthday cake, don't forget the candles!

ALL ABOUT JOY

Joy with her family. From the left: sister Launa, Joy, mom Patty, sister Lauren, and dad Cliff (1991)

Joy Wilson was born and raised in Los Angeles, California, and has been baking since she was a little girl. She is well known for her daily dabbles in butter and sugar as Joy the Baker.

Joy is a 100% taste buds–taught baker obsessed with butter, sugar, cream, and dark chocolate. Since 2008, she has shared her comforting and easy-to-follow recipes through her popular blog, joythebaker.com, inspiring home cooks of all ages.

Joy on her fifth birthday w her "hand" cake (1986)

Joy is a baking instructor, the author of three cookbooks, and editor-in-chief of *Joy the Baker* magazine. In all of her work, Joy proves baking is all about stepping into the kitchen with a monster sweet tooth and whipping up something that makes you want to lick your fingers and smile.

Joy the Baker fans at her first book signing (2012)

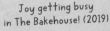
Joy getting busy in The Bakehouse! (2019)

Joy has transformed her home in Texas into a kitchen studio called "The Bakehouse." In this kitchen she tests recipes and holds weekly in-person and virtual baking workshops for students from around the United States.

She has won many awards for her online work and has been featured in some of the most prestigious newspapers and magazines in the world. She has also appeared on national TV shows and at food events.

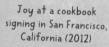
Joy at a cookbook signing in San Francisco, California (2012)

You can keep up with Joy's baking adventures on her blog and on Instagram. On any given day she can be found with a bag of freshly baked cookies and a big block of butter in her handbag.

Joy on *Entertainment Tonight* with Mario Lopez (2023)

GLOSSARY

Beating: mixing ingredients in a vigorous, regular motion

Bundt cake: a cake shaped like a ring, baked in a special ridged pan

Cake batter: the mixture of cake ingredients, before it goes in the oven to bake

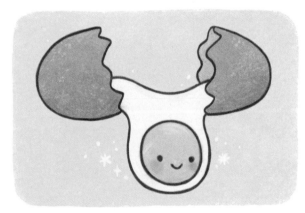

Cracking eggs: opening an eggshell to release the egg inside—while trying not to let any shell fall into the mixture

Creaming: blending soft butter and sugar together until pale and fluffy

Cup (c): a unit of measurement for liquid and solid ingredients

Dough: the mixture of ingredients for bakes such as bread, pastry, and cookies, before they go in the oven

Gram (g): a unit of measurement, mainly for solid ingredients

Greasing and flouring: rubbing butter inside of a cake pan, then shaking flour around the pan to coat the butter; ensures the cake will come out of the pan without sticking after it is baked

Ingredients: the wet and dry items that are put together in a recipe

Milliliter (ml): a unit of measurement for liquid ingredients

Ounce (oz): a unit of measurement for solid ingredients

Raising agents: ingredients that help a bake to rise when heated in the oven

Recipe: a list of ingredients and a friendly guide on how to bring them together

Room temperature: a warmer temperature outside of the fridge, used for ingredients in some recipes to create the right scientific reactions in the oven

Sieve: a bowl-shaped tool with a fine wire or plastic mesh

Sifting: shaking a powdered ingredient through a sieve to break up lumps into fine grains

Tablespoon (tbsp): a unit of measurement; greater than a teaspoon

Teaspoon (tsp): a unit of measurement; less than a tablespoon

 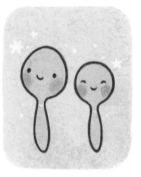

Whisking: mixing ingredients to add air and make the batter light, or to make sure they are thoroughly combined

Wire rack: a raised rack onto which a bake can be placed to cool evenly, due to air circulation on all sides

To my mom, Patty, who always inspires me
to be the best version of myself
JW

To my mum, Larisa, who showed me
how to make delicious things out of nothing
TK

To my dear mother, Drucilla, my inspiration
CW

**MAGIC CAT
PUBLISHING**

The illustrations were created digitally.
Set in Calder and Vodka Sans.

Library of Congress Control Number 2023952523
ISBN 978-1-4197-7607-6

Cover © 2024 Magic Cat
Text © 2024 Joy Wilson
Illustrations © 2024 Tatiana Kamshilina
Book design by Stephanie Jones

First published in the United Kingdom in 2024 by Magic Cat.
First published in North America in 2024 by Magic Cat, an imprint of ABRAMS.
All rights reserved. No portion of this book may be reproduced, stored in a
retrieval system, or transmitted in any form or by any means, mechanical,
electronic, photocopying, recording, or otherwise, without written permission
from the publisher.

Printed and bound in China
10 9 8 7 6 5 4 3 2 1

Abrams books are available at special discounts when purchased in quantity for
premiums and promotions as well as fundraising or educational use
as well as fundraising or educational use. Special editions can also be created to
specification. For details, contact specialsales@abramsbooks.com
or the address below.

FURTHER READING

**The Big, Fun Kids Baking Book: 110+ Recipes
for Young Bakers** by Food Network Magazine

**The Complete Baking Book for Young Chefs:
100+ Sweet and Savory Recipes that You'll
Love to Bake, Share & Eat!** by America's Test
Kitchen Kids

**Kid Chef Junior Bakes: My First Kids
Baking Cookbook** by Charity Mathews

**Recipes for Change: 12 Dishes Inspired by
a Year in Black History** by Michael Platt,
illustrated by Alleanna Harris

MIX
Paper | Supporting
responsible forestry
FSC® C144853
www.fsc.org

ABRAMS The Art of Books
195 Broadway, New York, NY 10007
abramsbooks.com

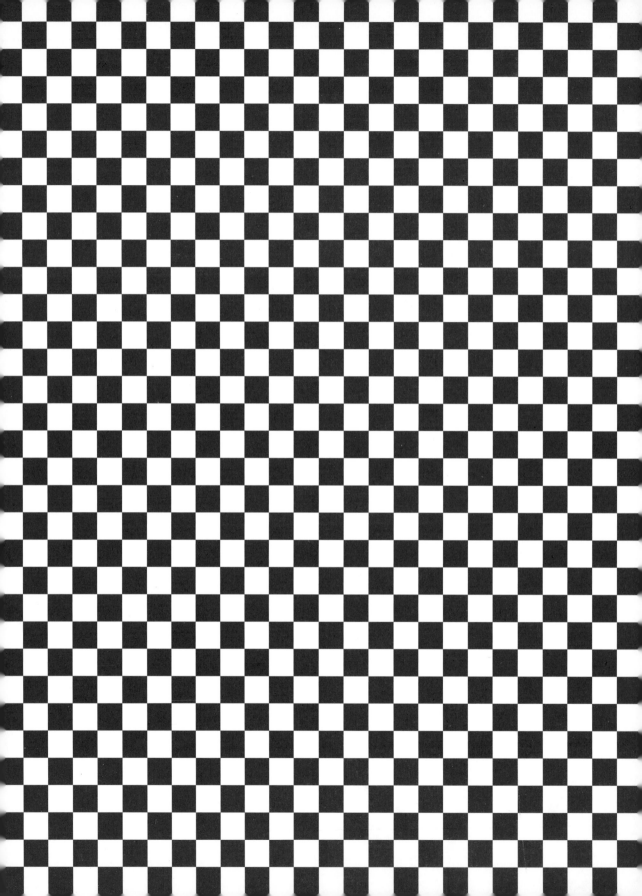